Original title:
Veil of Dreams

Copyright © 2024 Creative Arts Management OÜ
All rights reserved.

Author: Jude Lancaster
ISBN HARDBACK: 978-9916-90-096-3
ISBN PAPERBACK: 978-9916-90-097-0

The Cloak of Slumber

In twilight's embrace, shadows play,
Gentle whispers guide the way.
Dreams unfurl on night's soft breeze,
Wrapped in comfort, hearts find ease.

Stars twinkle bright, a soothing sight,
In the silence, spirits take flight.
Softly weaving through the night,
The cloak of slumber feels so right.

Lullabies in the Mist

A melody flows in the fog,
Echoes dance where shadows jog.
Night blooms softly, a calming sound,
In the mist, sweet dreams are found.

With whispers low and voices clear,
Lullabies wrap those we hold dear.
Through the haze, soft notes arise,
In the night, love never dies.

Reveries of the Cosmos

Stars collide in a cosmic waltz,
Planets spin, defying faults.
Galaxies drift in endless space,
Time a dancer, full of grace.

In dreams we soar to realms unknown,
With stardust paths we are shown.
Whispers echo through the void,
In reveries, hearts are buoyed.

Starlit Visions

Beneath the sky, where dreams ignite,
Starlit visions dance in the night.
Each spark a wish, a hope held tight,
In the cosmos, our souls take flight.

Waves of light in the velvet dark,
Illuminate moments, leave a mark.
Guided by constellations bright,
Together we chase eternal light.

Cascade of Enchanted Reveries

Whispers of dreams in twilight's glow,
Winding through forests where fairies flow.
Moonlit streams with secrets dance,
In this realm of enchanted chance.

Glistening petals, soft caress,
Stars above in a velvet dress.
Laughter echoes, a sweet embrace,
Magic lingers in every place.

Softly we drift on a silken breeze,
Carried away by the rustling leaves.
With every heartbeat, stories unfold,
In a cascade of wonders untold.

Chasing the Silhouettes of Tomorrow

In the fading light, shadows play,
Leading us forth into the fray.
Chasing the dreams that dance in sight,
Guided by hopes, shining bright.

Each step forward, a whisper of fate,
Echoes of laughter, we ride the bait.
With every heartbeat, we race the dawn,
Chasing silhouettes 'til the night is gone.

Fragments of wishes drift through the air,
Fueling the fire of dreams we share.
Every turn holds a path to explore,
Chasing the future, forevermore.

Threads of Illusion in the Dark

In shadows deep where illusions weave,
Mysteries linger, few dare believe.
Threads of silence entwined with night,
Whispers of secrets hidden from sight.

Flickers of light, a ghostly dance,
Enticing hearts with a daring chance.
Weaving through realms of sighs and fears,
Illusions shimmer, dissolving tears.

Beneath the surface, the truth resides,
In a tapestry where darkness hides.
With every thread, a story unfurls,
In the depths of shadowed worlds.

Woven Hopes of the Midnight Hour

Underneath the starlit sky,
Woven hopes begin to fly.
In the silence, hearts align,
Mirroring dreams that intertwine.

The clock ticks on in soft refrain,
Drifting gently like a sweet rain.
Every wish a spark of light,
Guiding us through the velvet night.

As moonbeams cast their silvery glow,
We gather dreams, allowing them to flow.
In this sacred space, we find our power,
Woven hopes bloom in the midnight hour.

Enigma of the Twilight

Twilight whispers secrets low,
In shadows where the soft winds blow.
Colors blend in soft embrace,
A mystery time cannot erase.

Stars awaken, shy and bright,
Guiding dreams into the night.
Flickers of a haunting past,
In each heartbeat, shadows cast.

Echoes dance on silent air,
Moments captured, rare and rare.
As darkness wraps the world in grace,
We find solace in this place.

The Sphere of Sleep

In the sphere where shadows play,
Whispers weave through night and day.
Dreams like stars begin to twine,
In quiet realms where hearts align.

Gentle sighs of soft repose,
Kisses brushed by evening's glow.
Floating on the clouds of thought,
Lost in moments time forgot.

Cradled in the arms of night,
We discover hidden light.
In this sphere where dreams are spun,
Awakened souls become as one.

The Mists of Becoming

Through mists that swirl and softly play,
We find our paths, come what may.
Each breath a step, a chance to grow,
In the dance of the ebb and flow.

Voices call from depths unseen,
Guiding hearts through spaces between.
In the haze of endless change,
Life unfolds, both wild and strange.

The dawn will break, a canvas bright,
Painting hopes in shades of light.
Embrace the journey, rise and sing,
For in the mists, the soul takes wing.

Night's Enigmatic Gift

Night descends with velvet grace,
Gifting dreams a sacred space.
Underneath the starlit dome,
Every heart begins to roam.

Secrets murmur in the dark,
Flickering like a distant spark.
In this solitude, we find,
The whispers of the cosmic kind.

Beneath the moon's soft, watchful gaze,
We wander through a mystic haze.
Night's embrace, so warm, so deep,
Tells us truths before we sleep.

Canvas of the Unconscious

Brush strokes dance on hidden dreams,
Colors whisper in muted screams,
Shapes emerge from twilight's haze,
Life's mysteries in a chromatic blaze.

Veiled secrets in every hue,
Unraveled tales that feel so true,
Infinite depths, a wondrous sea,
Art unveils what's meant to be.

Floating on Moonbeams

Gentle tides in silver light,
Whispers of the stars so bright,
Softly drifting, lose the way,
Embracing dreams till break of day.

Cradled on the night's embrace,
Time stands still in timeless space,
Every flicker holds a wish,
In moonlit magic, hearts can swish.

Pictures in the Dark

Shadows flicker, tales untold,
Fragments of a heart of gold,
Silent moments, memories spark,
Reflecting dreams within the dark.

Ink-black canvases, vivid sights,
Whispers of forgotten nights,
Every heartbeat, every sigh,
In the dark, our spirits fly.

Mirage of the Heart

Waves of longing touch the shore,
A fleeting glimpse we can't ignore,
Illusions dance on golden sand,
The truth we seek slips through our hands.

Shimmering hopes, a tender tease,
In the distance, love does breeze,
Chasing visions, lost and found,
The heart's mirage, forever bound.

The Murmurs of Spirit

In quiet woods where shadows play,
Whispers of leaves guide the way.
A gentle breeze, a soft refrain,
Nature's voice in sweet domain.

The brook sings low with secrets kept,
In twilight's glow, the earth has wept.
Echoes dance beneath the trees,
Carried softly on the breeze.

In the stillness, truths arise,
Stars reflect in lover's eyes.
Each moment paused, a breath of grace,
Where spirit meets in time and space.

Embrace the night, let worries flee,
Listen closely, and you may see.
The murmurings of soul's delight,
In every shadow, find the light.

Realms of Soft Light

In dawn's embrace, the world awakes,
Golden rays on silver lakes.
Petals glisten, soft and bright,
Catching dreams in realms of light.

Through misty veils of morning's breath,
The land rejoices, defying death.
Whispers of hope in colors spun,
Emerge anew with each rising sun.

A tapestry of shining hues,
Each thread a tale, a path to choose.
In quiet corners, magic stirs,
As nature sings, our spirit purrs.

With every step, the shadows fade,
In realms of light, our fears elayed.
We dance among the glowing beams,
In this soft space, we cultivate dreams.

Beyond the Umbra

In shadowed depths where secrets lie,
The heart beats fierce, the soul will fly.
Beyond the veil, a world of pain,
Awaits the light to break the chain.

The umbra casts a fleeting shade,
Yet in its dark, our strength is made.
Each struggle faced, a lesson learned,
From ashes rise, our spirits burned.

Hope flickers like a distant star,
Guiding us through paths bizarre.
In trials met, we find our way,
Beyond the umbra, light holds sway.

Embrace the dark, for it will teach,
The deepest truths that we can reach.
With courage as our steadfast guide,
Together we'll walk, side by side.

The Dreamscape Chronicles

In twilight realms where visions roam,
The dreamscape weaves a mystic home.
With silken threads of memory spun,
Awakening tales of who we've run.

Through landscapes vast and colors bright,
Echoes whisper in the night.
Adventures born from slumber's fate,
Unfolding pathways to create.

In every dream, a story waits,
Of joy and sorrow, love, and fates.
A canvas painted by the mind,
Where all our lost hopes are aligned.

As dawn approaches, dreams take flight,
Into the arms of morning light.
Yet in our hearts, those chronicles stay,
Guiding us on our waking way.

The Tender Glow

In dawn's embrace, a gentle light,
Softly breaks the bonds of night.
Petals open, and softly sigh,
As the world awakens, time slips by.

Golden rays through branches weave,
A canvas bright, we dare believe.
With every hue, the heart will dance,
In that sweet moment, we find our chance.

Whispers linger in the air,
Promises made without a care.
Nature's song, a siren's call,
In the tender glow, we find it all.

As shadows fade, the day will bloom,
Filling hearts, dispelling gloom.
In every glance, a story told,
In the tender glow, our souls behold.

Through the Guise of Night

Veils of darkness softly fall,
As stars emerge, they gently call.
The moonlit path begins to gleam,
Guiding dreamers through the stream.

Whispers echo in the hush,
Where time stands still, and shadows rush.
Secrets dance in silver light,
Through the guise of tranquil night.

Eyes reflect the cosmos wide,
In that embrace, we can confide.
Lost in wonder, hearts take flight,
Through the veil of calming night.

With each heartbeat, starlight flows,
Eternity because it knows.
In night's embrace, we find our sight,
Wrapped in dreams, through the guise of night.

Whispers of the Celestial

Above us sings the evening sky,
A canvas where the spirits fly.
Stars align in radiant streams,
Whispers drift through cosmic dreams.

Galaxies swirl in an endless dance,
Each twinkling light, a fleeting chance.
Echoes of a timeless past,
In celestial realms, our hopes hold fast.

Comets blaze with fiery tails,
Carrying secrets of ancient trails.
Through the vastness, our souls connect,
In whispers of love, we reflect.

Cosmic tides, they pull us near,
In the night's embrace, we persevere.
With every beat, our hearts entwine,
In whispers of the celestial, we shine.

A Symphony of Shadows

In twilight's hush, the shadows rise,
Crafting tales beneath the skies.
Silent whispers, a haunting tune,
As darkness dances with the moon.

Echoes call from deep within,
A melody where dreams begin.
With each note, the spirits sway,
In a symphony that won't decay.

Branches sway, the gentle breeze,
Carries secrets through the trees.
Lost in rhythm, we find our way,
In the music of shadows, we stay.

Each shadow weaves a story grand,
In twilight's grasp, we understand.
Together bound, we shall not part,
In a symphony of shadows, we heart.

Luminous Haze

In the dawn's gentle light,
Mist dances on the field.
Whispers of the night fade,
Dreams softly revealed.

Glowing warmth wraps the air,
Colors start to bloom.
Nature sings a soft tune,
Harmonies consume.

Each ray a golden thread,
Stitched through leaf and flower.
In this luminous haze,
We find our hidden power.

Fantasies Adrift

Drifting on a breeze,
Thoughts become the clouds.
Whirling through the sky,
An escape from the crowds.

With every fleeting dream,
We chase the unknown.
In worlds of fantasy,
Seeds of hope are sown.

Stars twinkle above,
Guiding every wish.
In night's quiet embrace,
We find our hearts' wish.

Lost in reverie,
Time stands still around.
With fantasies adrift,
We soar without bounds.

Echoes in the Twilight

As the day starts to fade,
Whispers of dusk arise.
Shadows stretch their limbs,
Painting darkening skies.

Footsteps softly trace paths,
Where secrets intertwine.
In the hush of twilight,
Lost moments align.

Stars begin their dance,
Lighting the velvet night.
Echoes in the twilight,
Call souls to take flight.

Dreams woven in silence,
Await morning's embrace.
In the twilight's soft glow,
We cherish time and space.

Silken Traces

In the moon's gleaming light,
Soft fabrics of the night.
Each whisper of the wind,
Leaves behind silken traces.

Through gardens of the mind,
Threads of thought intertwine.
A tapestry of dreams,
Woven with gentle care.

Petals fall like snowflakes,
Drifting on quiet streams.
Carried by a whisper,
Filling our heart with dreams.

In the twilight's embrace,
Every moment we find,
Silken traces of love,
Eternal, unconfined.

Secrets Beneath the Stars

Whispers in the midnight air,
Secrets hide beyond our stare.
Stars above, a silver sheen,
Hiding truths we've never seen.

In the dark, our dreams unfold,
Fables whispered, tales retold.
Constellations guide our way,
Leading hearts that yearn to sway.

Beneath the moon's enchanting light,
Shadows dance in the quiet night.
Mysteries woven, soft and deep,
In the cosmos, secrets sleep.

Each twinkle holds a hidden sigh,
A promise bound to never die.
Wanderers gaze, with hope anew,
For in the stars, we find our view.

Ethereal Reflections

Mirrored worlds in twilight's glow,
Thoughts like ripples, soft and slow.
Glimmers dance upon the stream,
Awakening a distant dream.

In the silence, echoes roam,
Whispers finding their way home.
Softly bound by time and space,
Every glance, a sweet embrace.

Reflections paint the skies so vast,
Moments cherished, shadows cast.
Each ripple tells a story true,
Of fleeting days and skies so blue.

Waves of wonder touch the soul,
In peace and calm, we become whole.
Ethereal visions reign so clear,
In every heart, they draw us near.

Chasing the Horizon

Beyond the hills where dreams arise,
Endless beauty paints the skies.
A journey starts with every breath,
Chasing light, defying death.

Wanderlust ignites the spark,
Drawing seekers from the dark.
Every step, a tale unfolds,
In the warmth, the heart beholds.

The horizon calls, a siren's plea,
With open arms, it welcomes me.
Each sunset brings a brand new fight,
Guided forward by the light.

As colors blend in evening's hush,
The soul awakens with a rush.
Chasing dreams both near and far,
Forever guided by the stars.

Night's Gentle Caress

Veils of dusk, a soft embrace,
Whispers cradle, time slows its pace.
Stars emerge in velvet skies,
A lullaby that never dies.

Clouds drift gently, dreams take flight,
Bathed in silver, pure delight.
Moonlight weaves a silken thread,
Kissing softly, dreams are fed.

In the quiet, hearts beat slow,
Night's gentle caress, a loving flow.
Every moment, still and clear,
In the dark, our hopes draw near.

As dawn peeks with a tender glow,
Night's secrets blend with morning's flow.
Grateful hearts for night's embrace,
In its arms, we find our place.

Secrets of the Gloom

In the heart of night, whispers call, Secrets hidden, shadows fall. Moonlight glimmers on the lake, Truths and myths, a gentle wake.

Fog drapes softly, veils of gray, What lies beyond, we dare not say. Silence wraps the restless mind, In the gloom, what truths we find.

Footsteps echo on the ground, In this hush, no one is found. Every secret, a story's thread, In the shadows, we're all led.

As dawn approaches, fears subside, In twilight's glow, they turn the tide. Secrets linger, but fade away, In light's embrace, we greet the day.

Awakening in Shadows

Beneath the stars, a world unfolds, In quiet sighs, the night is bold. Shadows stretching, softly dance, Awakened dreams in twilight's trance.

The clock ticks slow, as whispers grow, Secrets hidden, we yearn to know. Grains of time slip through our hands, In shadows' depth, our heart expands.

A flicker here, a shiver there, In silence, we breathe the midnight air. Each shadow cast tells tales anew, In night's embrace, we find what's true.

With dawn's soft light, the shadows fade, But in our hearts, their echoes stayed. Awoken now, we face the sun, In every shadow, we are one.

Gleaming Dreams

In the quiet night, dreams take flight, Gleaming visions, pure and bright. Stars like candles in the dark, Each a wish, each a spark.

Whispers woven in the air, Floating lightly, without care. Hearts are racing, spirits soar, Through the silence, we explore.

Reflections on a silver stream, A world alive with every dream. Chasing shadows, catching light, In gleaming dreams, we find our sight.

With morning's breath, we softly wake, The dreams remain, a gentle ache. They guide our path, our hearts ignite, In every gleam, we seek the light.

Twilight Musings

As twilight falls, the day retreats, In the stillness, the heart beats. Thoughts like whispers in the breeze, Twilight musings bring us ease.

Colors blend, a canvas wide, Beneath the sky, our hopes reside. In the dusk, we find our way, Musing dreams of yesterday.

The world slows down, a gentle pause, In twilight's glow, we find our cause. Each moment cherished, softly spins, In the twilight, life begins.

As night descends, stars appear, A symphony of dreams lies near. In shadows' arms, we softly sway, Twilight musings guide our way.

The Fabric of Forgotten Desires

Threads of longing weave through night,
Whispers lost in shadows' flight.
Hidden dreams that softly sigh,
Cloaked in silence, time slips by.

Echoes of what once could be,
Fleeting glimpses, memory's key.
Woven tales in fibers old,
Stories of yearning, softly told.

In the corners of the mind,
Desires linger, undefined.
Fingers trace the patterns worn,
In the fabric, passion's sworn.

Yet, in twilight, they unfold,
Colors bright, then shades of gold.
Forgotten hopes in twilight's glow,
In the heart, the fabric grows.

Enchanted Worlds Beyond the Gaze

Beyond the hills, where visions dart,
Lies a land that stirs the heart.
Forests whisper secrets low,
Rivers dance in moonlit glow.

Faeries flit on wings of light,
Guiding dreams through starry night.
Mountains rise with ageless grace,
In their shadows, time's embrace.

Gentle breezes, soft and sweet,
Carry tales on currents fleet.
In this realm, where souls align,
Every moment feels divine.

Violet skies and emerald fields,
To longing hearts, their magic yields.
Here, the world is pure and free,
In each breath, eternity.

A Journey Through Celestial Mists

Step into realms where starlight plays,
Hidden paths in the cosmic haze.
Footprints left in galaxies bright,
Wonders dance in the silent night.

Misty veils of forgotten dreams,
Flow in rivers of shimmering beams.
Hearts take flight on astral wings,
Lost among the songs of things.

Galaxies whisper tales untold,
Of journeys brave, of destinies bold.
In the expanse, where echoes sigh,
Time bends low, as moments fly.

Drifting through the cosmic stream,
Each heartbeat, a radiant dream.
In the mist, truths are sought,
A journey through the thoughts we caught.

Timeless Echoes of Heavens Unknown

In the stillness, a voice calls clear,
Leading seekers to what is dear.
Beyond the stars, where shadows blend,
Timeless echoes shall never end.

Each moment caught in twilight's grace,
Reflects the heart's enduring trace.
Waves of time, they ebb and flow,
Infinite paths for us to know.

Whispers dance through ages past,
In every heartbeat, memories cast.
From ancient skies to futures bright,
Heavens weave our shared light.

Echoes linger, soft and sweet,
In the silence, our souls meet.
Timeless echoes, forever spun,
Binding us till time is done.

Whispers of Moonlit Shadows

In the night, shadows sway,
Beneath the moon's gentle light.
Whispers dance on soft breeze,
Carrying secrets from night.

Stars blink above in delight,
Their stories, a cosmic song.
Branches sway, a sweet embrace,
Nature's rhythm, where we belong.

Echoes of dreams softly beam,
As the world fades into grey.
In these whispers of moonlit dreams,
We find solace, come what may.

Slumber comes, like a tide,
Drawing us into its fold.
In shadows, we find our peace,
The night's embrace, tender and bold.

Tapestry of Slumbering Hues

Colors weave in soft twilight,
Binding day to night's gentle kiss.
Tapestries of dreams ignite,
In the silence, we find bliss.

Various shades of whispered hopes,
Paint the sky with stories untold.
As the universe gently gropes,
With threads of silver, bright and bold.

Night blooms with a vibrant sigh,
Each hue a memory, a sigh.
In this quiet, souls can fly,
Beneath the vast, starry sky.

Dreams embrace in pastel glow,
As slumber's lullaby takes hold.
In this tapestry, we flow,
With slumbering hues, bright and gold.

Ethereal Echoes of Night

Silken whispers carve the dark,
Ethereal echoes take flight.
As the moon ignites a spark,
Guiding dreams into the night.

Footsteps soft on dew-kissed grass,
The world embraces the unseen.
In this space, where shadows pass,
We find solace, serene and keen.

Every breath a fleeting thought,
In the quiet, secrets flow.
Ethereal echoes are caught,
In the stillness, time moves slow.

Stars shimmer in the vast expanse,
Each twinkle a soft, knowing word.
In this ethereal dance and glance,
Night's echoes whisper, seldom heard.

Shrouded Fantasies in Twilight

Twilight wraps the world in gray,
As day surrenders to night's call.
Fantasies emerge, bright display,
In shadows that comfortably fall.

Veils of mystery softly rise,
As dreams spill out from hidden lore.
In the stillness, the heart replies,
To night's promise, forevermore.

Whispers swirl in playful jest,
Tales of wonder, ridden with grace.
In the twilight, we find our rest,
As fantasies twirl in soft embrace.

With each star, a story unfurls,
In the twilight's gleaming hue.
Shrouded fantasies of the worlds,
Inviting our spirits to renew.

Enchanted Snooze

In a world where dreams do bloom,
Soft whispers float in the room.
Moonlight dances on your face,
Time stands still in this embrace.

Clouds of cotton, pure and white,
Cradling souls in gentle night.
Stars above begin to gleam,
Swaying softly in a dream.

Tucked in close, the shadows fade,
A haven in this twilight shade.
Here, the heart learns how to rest,
In slumber's soft, enchanted nest.

Serene Illusions

Misty trails of silver light,
Lead us softly through the night.
Glimmers of a distant star,
Guide us gently, near and far.

Whispers float on midnight air,
Carried stories, sweet and rare.
Lullabies that cradle dreams,
Wrapped in warmth, their soft moonbeams.

Flowers bloom in velvet dark,
Where silence praises every spark.
Let go of the worries' weight,
Embrace this peaceful, woven state.

Ethereal Reverie

In twilight's grasp, the echoes rise,
A symphony of soft goodbyes.
Dreamers tread on starry paths,
Painting worlds with gentle laughs.

Fleeting thoughts like clouds drift by,
Whispering secrets to the sky.
Every moment, pure and bright,
In this space of endless light.

Time relents to gentle sway,
As night unfolds, swept away.
Floating where the heart can see,
In this ethereal reverie.

Slumber's Embrace

Cradled in the arms of night,
Dreams take flight and hearts ignite.
Whispers of a lullaby,
Drift across the darkened sky.

With every breath, the world cocooned,
In silken sheets, where peace is tuned.
Every fear, a shadow cast,
In slumber's hold, a spell is cast.

Close your eyes, let worries fade,
In this tranquil, still parade.
Comforted by night's sweet grace,
Find your peace in slumber's embrace.

Faded Memories

Whispers of laughter fade away,
Shadows dance where we used to play.
Pictures drawn in sepia tones,
Echoes linger, haunting our bones.

Ghosts of moments lose their light,
Fading softly into the night.
Time unwinds its fragile thread,
Memories drift like words unsaid.

Familiar paths now overgrown,
In silent corners, seeds are sown.
Once bright colors now dim and grey,
Faded memories, they slip away.

Phosphorescent Daydreams

Beneath a sky of swirling hues,
Imagination begins to muse.
Sparkling thoughts take flight at dusk,
In twilight's fold, they breathe and husk.

Crystalline worlds in shadows gleam,
Mingled with a phosphorescent dream.
Boundless whispers, soft and clear,
Call through the night, inviting cheer.

Fleeting visions kiss the dark,
Glowing softly, they leave a mark.
In this realm where dreams convene,
Life unfolds, a shimmering scene.

The Softness of Night

Velvet skies embrace the stars,
In tranquil hush, the world is ours.
Moonlit beams on gentle streams,
Flowing whispers, sweet, like dreams.

Softened edges of day's demands,
Crickets sing in gentle bands.
A lullaby to ease the fray,
In the quiet, night will stay.

Stars blink softly, a gentle sigh,
As shadows weave, the night slips by.
In this softness, we find our peace,
Where all our worries fade, release.

Hidden Realms

Beyond the veil of daily sights,
Lie hidden realms, enchanted nights.
Whispers beckon through the trees,
Secrets carried on the breeze.

In tangled roots and ancient lore,
Mysteries wait, forevermore.
With every rustle, worlds collide,
In hidden realms, the magic hides.

Softly spoken spells of grace,
In forgotten paths, we find our place.
Exploring shadows, light entwined,
In hidden realms, the heart aligned.

Whispered Melodies

In the quiet night, whispers flow,
Soft notes dance in the gentle glow.
Every shadow hums a tune,
Beneath the watchful, silver moon.

Hearts entwine with every breeze,
Carrying love through swaying trees.
Melodies weave through the dark,
Igniting sparks, a glowing mark.

Each sigh a sound, each breath a song,
In this embrace, we both belong.
The cadence of time gently sways,
Carving our dreams in unison's ways.

As dawn draws near, the whispers fade,
But in our hearts, the memories stayed.
A shared harmony that won't depart,
The whispered melodies of the heart.

A Tapestry of Stars

Underneath the vast, cosmic skies,
A tapestry where wonder lies.
Stars like threads, woven bright,
Each glimmer a tale in the night.

Constellations tell of old lore,
Whispers of dreams we can't ignore.
Galaxies swirl in a delicate dance,
Inviting stargazers into a trance.

With every twinkle, a secret shared,
Stories of lovers, and dreams declared.
In the depth, we search for fate,
In the silence, we contemplate.

A celestial symphony above,
Woven together with hope and love.
As the night unfolds, we stand in awe,
A tapestry of stars that leaves us raw.

Moonlit Whispers

In the silvery glow of the night,
Whispers linger, soft and light.
Moonbeams lace the tranquil scene,
Magic unfolds where we have been.

Secrets carried on the breeze,
A gentle sigh among the trees.
Every flicker a heart's desire,
Igniting warmth, a quiet fire.

Beneath the stars, our shadows merge,
In the stillness, emotions surge.
We share our dreams with moonlit eyes,
Under the veil of endless skies.

In this moment, time stands still,
In whispered tones, we feel the thrill.
Wrapped in night, we softly sway,
As moonlit whispers guide our way.

The Art of Sleep

In the cocoon of twilight's embrace,
Dreams unfold, a gentle space.
With each sigh, the world subsides,
As comfort wraps and softly guides.

Slumber weaves a soothing thread,
Where worries pause and silence spreads.
In starlit corners, the mind takes flight,
Painting scenes in the depth of night.

Rest, dear soul, let the day unwind,
In the realm where peace is kind.
Embrace the calm, let go of strife,
Discover the art that breathes new life.

As dawn approaches, dreams will linger,
A tender touch of night's soft finger.
In the art of sleep, we find our way,
A journey renewed with each new day.

Heirs to the Night

In shadows deep, the secrets lie,
Beneath the stars, the whispers sigh.
We dance where time begins to fade,
Heirs to the night, our hearts persuade.

Through velvet skies, our spirits soar,
Unraveling dreams from the ancient lore.
With every breath, the darkness blooms,
Embracing us in midnight's rooms.

The moonlight paints our silent oath,
A tapestry of fate and growth.
With open hands, we greet the dusk,
In shadows cast, we find our trust.

Awake, we wander, lost in flight,
In the quiet realms of endless night.
The cosmos calls, we heed the plight,
Together, we are heirs to night.

Flashes of the Infinite

In fleeting moments, time stands still,
A spark ignites, a dream to fulfill.
Through galaxies bright, our minds expand,
Flashes of the infinite at hand.

Eternal echoes of wild delight,
Dance with the stars in the velvet night.
Each heartbeat pulses with colors bold,
Stories of wonders, past and untold.

Perception shifts like sand on the shore,
With every blink, we see so much more.
Veils of the past lift gently away,
As flashes of the infinite play.

We reach for dreams that light the way,
Guided by flashes that never decay.
In this vast cosmos, our spirits roam,
In unity found, we create a home.

The Silk of Spacetime

Threads intertwine in the cosmic loom,
Woven together, we banish the gloom.
The silk of spacetime, fine and bright,
Holds the fabric of day and night.

Each moment a stitch in the grand design,
Connecting our fates, your hand in mine.
Through ripples of time, we start to see,
The beauty in chaos, a tapestry.

With whispers of stars resonating near,
We dance on the edges of hope and fear.
In the quiet hush, we find our place,
In the silk of spacetime, we embrace.

Woven in love, our stories blend,
In the strands of destiny, we transcend.
Together we journey, forever aligned,
In the silk of spacetime, hearts intertwined.

Ascent into Dreams

From whispered thoughts, we take our flight,
Ascending slowly into the night.
In realms of slumber, we intertwine,
Ascent into dreams, your soul with mine.

Mountains of hope rise in the mist,
With every crest, we feel the bliss.
Through valleys deep of twilight's hue,
We chase the dreams that feel so true.

With wings of starlight, we break the dawn,
In the quiet spaces, we linger on.
Exploring horizons that shimmer bright,
Ascent into dreams, a wondrous sight.

In this sacred dance, we lose our way,
Yet find our hearts where the shadows play.
Together we soar, united, it seems,
In the echoing void of our dreams.

Lullabies Beneath Starlit Canopies

Soft whispers weave through the night,
Dreams take flight on silver wings.
Crickets sing their gentle tune,
While moonlight dances, softly clings.

Clouds drift slowly, a velvet sea,
Cradling stars in a tender sway.
Serene sighs of the slumbering leaves,
Guide the weary hearts at play.

Shadows stretch in a silent sigh,
Each lullaby a soothing balm.
The world is hushed, in soft embrace,
Wrapped in night's enveloping calm.

Beneath the vast, celestial dome,
Rest your head and close your eyes.
In this cradle of whispered dreams,
Find the peace that never dies.

Mirage of the Wandering Mind

Thoughts like rivers twist and turn,
Flowing through the canyons deep.
Glimmers of hope dance and burn,
In the silence where secrets sleep.

Fleeting moments blur in haze,
Reality shifts with a gentle sigh.
Chasing shadows in endless maze,
Lost in visions that drift and fly.

Fragments linger, echoes of light,
Drawing paths that lead astray.
Yet in the chaos, a flicker bright,
Guides the heart toward the dawn of day.

Through the mirage, clarity shines,
Where whispers tell of the ethereal.
In the wanderer's realm, intertwines,
The essence of dreams made material.

Secrets Entwined in Gossamer Light

Whispers float on the evening breeze,
Secrets wrapped in shimmering strands.
Delicate truths dance with ease,
In the glow of twilight's lands.

The golden threads of laughter fade,
As shadows merge in a tender song.
Silent wishes in silence laid,
Gossamer dreams, where we belong.

Petals fall on the whispering ground,
Each revealing a tale untold.
In the stillness, mysteries abound,
Entwined in love that's pure as gold.

In the light of dusk's embrace,
Find the magic that softly glows.
With each secret, a soft trace,
Of all the places our spirit flows.

Embrace of the Sleepwalker's Path

Footsteps echo in twilight's veil,
Carried by dreams through the night.
A wanderer lost, yet never pale,
In the embrace of the stars' soft light.

Silhouettes move with grace and ease,
Guided by whispers of serene fate.
In the stillness, a gentle tease,
Awakens the heart to ruminate.

Each step leads to unseen lands,
Where shadows flicker, and silence sings.
In the dance of fate's gentle hands,
The sleepwalker sighs, as hope springs.

Trust the journey, though paths may wane,
In the dreams that the night has spun.
The embrace of the stars, without a stain,
Illuminates all that is yet to come.

The Never-Ending Tides of Dreamscape

In realms where visions softly sway,
The tides of dreams lead hearts away.
With waves of light that softly gleam,
We drift within a timeless dream.

The stars they whisper secrets true,
In colors bright of every hue.
Each heartbeat dances with the night,
While shadows dress the world in flight.

Beneath these skies of velvet blue,
We weave the tales the ancients knew.
In every sigh, a world unfolds,
Through threads of silver, fate beholds.

So let us sail on dreams so wide,
Through currents deep, where hopes reside.
With every turn, the waves will call,
To gather light, we rise and fall.

Songs of the Unspoken Realm

In silence where the secrets dwell,
The heart speaks softly, no need to tell.
Each echo paints the air with grace,
Where thoughts intertwine in sacred space.

The stars compose a silent tune,
As night wraps 'round beneath the moon.
In whispers held by gentle sighs,
The unspoken truth never dies.

Through shadows cast by fleeting light,
The soul will dance and take its flight.
Each note a bridge to worlds unseen,
In melodies both soft and keen.

So listen close, the songs we share,
In every heartbeat, everywhere.
The echoes of a realm so vast,
Revealing dreams that hold us fast.

Whispers of the Night

Beneath the cloak of midnight's veil,
The stars begin their whispered tale.
In shadows deep, where secrets hide,
The moonlight glimmers, quiet pride.

Each rustle through the ancient trees,
Brings gentle thoughts upon the breeze.
With every breath, a story spun,
In twilight's glow, we come undone.

The night unfolds its tender grace,
As starlit visions take their place.
In dreams we chase, our spirits soar,
To touch the sky, forevermore.

So linger in this sacred hour,
Embrace the night, its quiet power.
For every whisper softly shared,
Unlocks the light that we all dared.

Shimmering Shadows

In twilight's grip, the shadows dance,
With every step, a fleeting chance.
They shimmer softly, hint and tease,
In silvered light of whispered breeze.

The echoes of a world unknown,
Reflect the dreams we call our own.
In every corner, shadows play,
A graceful waltz, come what may.

Through whispered nights, we find our way,
As stars above begin to sway.
With every flicker, hope ignites,
In shimmering shadows, love delights.

So let us wander, hand in hand,
Through twilight trails, a dreamer's land.
For in the shadows, truths arise,
Illuminating hearts and skies.

Starlit Confessions

Under the sky, secrets unfold,
Whispers of dreams in silver and gold.
Hearts bare in the glow of the night,
Each star a wish, twinkling so bright.

Moonlight dances on tender skin,
Promises whispered, softly begin.
In the silence, truth takes flight,
Boundless love in starlit light.

The universe listens, we share our fears,
In cosmic arms, we dry our tears.
With every heartbeat, our stories blend,
Starlit confessions, where souls transcend.

As dusk surrenders to dawn's embrace,
Memories linger, a cherished trace.
Together we wander, hand in hand,
In starlit confessions, we understand.

The Aura of Sleep

The world dims down, a gentle sigh,
Embraced by dreams as night drifts by.
In the stillness, shadows creep,
Whispers echo in the aura of sleep.

Softly falling into the unknown,
A canvas of wishes, each heart a stone.
In twilight's hush, the spirit weeps,
Cradled softly in the aura of sleep.

Stars glimmer faintly, a distant call,
In quiet corners, we rise and fall.
While time stands still in a peaceful deep,
We find our solace in the aura of sleep.

Awake tomorrow with stories to tell,
Of enchanted realms where shadows dwell.
In night's embrace, our secrets keep,
Lost and found in the aura of sleep.

Whims of the Night

The night unfolds with a playful grin,
A canvas of dreams where adventures begin.
Stars play tag in the velvet sky,
As moonbeams wink with a gentle sigh.

Whispers of magic drift through the air,
Tales of wonder, a hidden affair.
Every breeze carries a secret delight,
In the charming whims of the night.

Laughter of crickets, a sweet serenade,
As shadows embrace, dreams softly invade.
In the orchestra of stars shining bright,
We dance to the whims of the night.

With every heartbeat, a story to tell,
In twilight's laughter, we cast a spell.
As dawn approaches, we hold on tight,
To the fleeting whims of the night.

Gossamer Wishes

On silken threads, our wishes weave,
In the quiet hour, we dare believe.
Delicate dreams carried by the breeze,
Tender whispers, sweet mysteries.

Gossamer hopes, fragile and bright,
In the heart's garden, we plant our light.
With every breath, we take our flight,
Chasing the dawn in the still of the night.

Each dewdrop holds a story untold,
In vibrant hues, the future unfolds.
Through shadows and light, we seek the bliss,
Lost in the magic of gossamer wishes.

With open hearts, we yearn to explore,
The beauty within and what lies in store.
In the quiet moments, dreams persist,
As we gather together, our gossamer wishes.

Luminous Nightscapes in the Mind

In shadows deep, the dreams arise,
Whispers dance beneath the skies.
Cascading lights, a shimmering stream,
Stars ignite the fold of dream.

Each twinkle brings a tale anew,
Of lands where hopes and memories grew.
In this vast expanse, we wander free,
Chasing echoes of what used to be.

Nightscapes weave a spectral thread,
Linking worlds where thoughts are fed.
Minds unbound, in restless flight,
Finding solace in the night.

A canvas dark, with colors bright,
Painting visions, pure delight.
In the stillness, visions gleam,
Luminous nightscapes fill the dream.

Charmed Slumbers and Ethereal Realities

In chambers soft, the quiet hums,
As slumber's dance gently drums.
Clouds of cotton, angels sing,
As twilight weaves her tender fling.

Ethereal realms where wishes float,
A soothing sigh, a silent note.
Touched by magic in the air,
We drift to lands that free us from care.

Charmed slumbers cradle the mind,
With whispers of dreams intertwined.
In the twilight, shadows gleam,
A tapestry spun from a dream.

Each heartbeat whispers a tale told,
In moonlight's grasp, the night is gold.
Through realms of wonder, we explore,
Charmed slumbers open the door.

Fluttering Delirium Amongst the Stars

In sleepless nights, the mind takes flight,
Chasing shadows, flickering light.
Delirium dances, wild and free,
Amongst the stars, just you and me.

Galaxies swirl in a cosmic embrace,
Each twinkling star holds a trace.
Fluttering visions, a ride through time,
Drifting along in playful rhyme.

Lost in the fabric of dreams untold,
A luminous chase, bright and bold.
Through nebulas of vibrant hues,
We weave our dreams, we lose the blues.

Together we float on celestial streams,
In the chorus of whispered dreams.
Fluttering hearts in the cosmic sea,
Amongst the stars, it's just you and me.

Reflections on the Edge of Sleep

On the brink where shadows play,
Reflections of night blend into day.
Eyes half-closed, worlds collide,
As the tide of dreams starts to glide.

Gentle whispers call us near,
Inviting soft imaginings clear.
In this liminal space, we dwell,
Stories beckon, a silent spell.

Each thought a ripple, a fleeting glance,
A dance with time in a twilight trance.
With every heartbeat, we softly creep,
In the silence that hangs on the edge of sleep.

Mirrors reflect what the heart conceives,
In the folds of dreams, the soul believes.
As the night wraps its arms so deep,
We find our peace on the edge of sleep.

Mystical Slumber

In twilight's embrace, dreams softly call,
Whispers of magic in the shadows fall.
Stars gently twinkle in the night's deep veil,
A world of wonder where secrets prevail.

Moonlight dances on the silent stream,
Floating on hope like a fragile dream.
Silken threads weave through the calm night air,
Lost in the realms of a lover's care.

Sleep's tender fingers touch every soul,
Cradling whispers that make us whole.
In the slumber's hold, we find our light,
Illuminated softly through the night.

A journey begun in the depths of sleep,
Into the unknown, our thoughts gently creep.
Mystical visions in the night emerge,
In slumber's embrace, our spirits surge.

Threads of Enchantment

In the loom of twilight, threads intertwine,
Colors of magic in a pattern divine.
Woven with care, each strand tells a tale,
Of whispered secrets in the moonlit trail.

Glimmers of starlight on gossamer lace,
Catch the soft breath of a dream's gentle grace.
Weaving the night with a touch of delight,
Embracing the shadows that dance in the light.

Crimson and gold in a tapestry spun,
Life's fleeting moments, one by one,
Each thread a wish on the winds of fate,
Binding our hearts in connections innate.

In the fabric of dreams, we find our way,
Guided by starlight through night into day.
Threads of enchantment in silence unfold,
A story of love that never grows old.

Midnight Fantasia

Under a sky where the wild dreams play,
Whispers of night beckon, gently sway.
Moonbeams weave through the tangled trees,
A symphony of shadows carried by the breeze.

Softly the night sings an ancient song,
In a realm of wonder, we all belong.
Stars twinkle like jewels, bright and bold,
Guiding our hearts through the night so cold.

Fantasia dances on the edge of sight,
Awakening magic in the heart of night.
Waves of euphoria in every breath,
Celebrating life, defying death.

In dreams, we wander through pathways unknown,
Discovering treasures in the seeds we've sown.
Midnight enfolds us, a blanket so deep,
Rocking our souls in the cradle of sleep.

The Ephemeral Drift

Like whispers carried on a gentle breeze,
Time flows softly, bending like the trees.
Moments float by like leaves on a stream,
Each a reflection of yesterday's dream.

In the ephemeral drift of passing days,
We chase the sun through its golden rays.
Memories flicker like fireflies bright,
Guiding us home through the shimmering night.

Change is a rhythm, a dance we embrace,
Carved in the heart, leaving delicate trace.
Life's fleeting beauty, a transient gift,
In every heartbeat, we quietly lift.

As shadows lengthen, the twilight appears,
We gather our stories, our hopes, and fears.
In the flow of existence, we find our way,
Embracing the magic of each passing day.

Mystical Fragments of Aether

In twilight's glow, the stars align,
Whispers weave a tale divine.
Veils of time, they softly part,
Guiding dreams that fill the heart.

Echoes rise from depths unknown,
In the silence, truths are sown.
Fragments dance in cosmic flight,
Shimmering through the endless night.

Glimmers spark in shadow's keep,
Awakening the souls that sleep.
Wisps of light, they tease the mind,
In the realm of the intertwined.

Stars converge, the night does sing,
A symphony of hope takes wing.
Each small breath a universe,
In the aether's gentle verse.

Shadows of a Thousand Whispers

In corners dark, where secrets dwell,
Shadows murmur, tales to tell.
Voices soft like autumn leaves,
Rustling through the webs of eves.

A thousand dreams in whispers pass,
Reflecting in the shattered glass.
Echoes fade, yet linger long,
Binding hearts to ancient song.

Flickering lights from far away,
Calling forth the break of day.
In the silence, truths emerge,
As shadows play, the spirits surge.

Underneath the silver moon,
Mysteries dance, they start to swoon.
In every breath, a tale is spun,
As darkness waits for morning sun.

The Quiet Dance of Shaded Thoughts

In spaces where the lost hearts meet,
Shaded thoughts in silence greet.
Quiet dances twirl in mind,
Echoes of the past aligned.

Moments drift like gentle streams,
Carrying the weight of dreams.
In stillness, visions intertwine,
Crafting shadows, soft and fine.

Every breath a step we take,
In the night, we're wide awake.
Waltzing through the velvet night,
Finding solace in the light.

As dawn awakens, fears take flight,
Leaving trails of yesterday's plight.
In the quiet dance, we find,
The sacred pulse of heart and mind.

Radiant Fables of Unseen Worlds

In the depths of night, tales unfold,
Radiant fables, stories bold.
Worlds unseen, they shimmer bright,
Bathed in the softest light.

Every whisper holds a dream,
Floating on a silver beam.
Time forgotten, lost in space,
Inviting all to find their place.

In the tapestry of the skies,
Colors blend with ancient sighs.
A dance of fate, a cosmic thread,
In every heart, the journey led.

With every star, a promise glows,
In the night, true magic flows.
Radiant fables weave anew,
Crafting worlds from dreams we pursue.

Untold Journeys

With every step, a tale unfolds,
Whispers of dreams in colors bold.
Paths that twist like rivers flow,
Secrets waiting, hearts in tow.

Mountains rise and valleys dip,
Carrying hopes, on this long trip.
Each shadow cast tells stories old,
A journey woven with threads of gold.

Footprints linger on the sand,
Echoes of time in distant lands.
Stars above, a guiding light,
Illuminating, the endless night.

In every sigh, a wish takes flight,
Painting dreams in the canvas of night.
A journey's heart beats with each sigh,
Embracing the dance of the unspoken sky.

Colors of Calm

Gentle hues of morning light,
Paint the world in soft delight.
Whispers of the evening breeze,
Bring a stillness, put the mind at ease.

Azure skies and fields of gold,
Stories of peace silently told.
Where the river meets the sea,
Harmony flows, wild and free.

Clouds drift lazily, soft and white,
A canvas stretched, an artist's sight.
In nature's arms, worries fade,
Rejuvenated, in colors laid.

As twilight descends, shadows blend,
The palette shifts, a perfect end.
In every breath, calmness we find,
A tranquil heart, and a peaceful mind.

Beyond the Serene Veil

Curtains drawn, a world concealed,
Whispers of dreams yet to be revealed.
Beyond the veil, where secrets lie,
A realm of wonder, beneath the sky.

Softly glimmers the distant light,
Guiding the lost through the night.
Each step taken, a heartbeats call,
To weave the fate of one and all.

Mysteries dance in celestial glow,
Promises hidden in the flow.
With every sigh, the truth unveils,
Beyond the calm of tranquil gales.

In the silence, wisdom speaks,
Through whispered joys, the soul it seeks.
A journey dear to those who dare,
To venture forth, beyond the air.

Wishful Wanderings

In dreams I wander, far and wide,
Seeking places where hopes abide.
Through meadows lush and mountains tall,
With every step, I hear their call.

A whispering breeze, a guiding sound,
Echoes of joy in leaps unbound.
With starlit skies, my heart takes flight,
In wishful wanderings, pure delight.

Time stands still in this sacred space,
A gentle smile upon my face.
Every corner, a new delight,
Painting the world in colors bright.

In the tapestry of lands unknown,
Adventure blooms, and dreams have grown.
With open arms, I'll chase the sun,
In wishful wanderings, forever run.

Veiled Imaginations in Starlit Realms

In the hush of night's embrace,
Whispers float like silver lace.
Dreams take flight on shadows' glow,
As the moon weaves tales below.

Stars hang low, a glimmering thread,
Painting visions in our head.
Veils of wonder softly part,
Kindling sparks within the heart.

Lost in thoughts, we drift afar,
Following each shimmering star.
In the depths of twilight's scheme,
We explore the fabric of dream.

Echoes of the night's refrains,
Dance upon these starlit plains.
In their light, we dare to roam,
Crafting wonders we call home.

Flickering Dreams on Gossamer Wings

In the twilight, soft and bright,
Dreams do shimmer, taking flight.
Gossamer wings upon the air,
Carrying hopes beyond despair.

Flickering thoughts, a gentle spark,
Guiding us through shadows dark.
With each flutter, joy be found,
In the realm where dreams abound.

Chasing whispers, light as air,
As the stars both shine and glare.
Moments woven in delight,
Taking shape within the night.

Hands reaching out, to grasp the real,
Feeling every vivid thrill.
On these wings, we soar and stream,
Embracing all our wildest dreams.

Pathways of the Half-Remembered

In the corridors of mind,
Echoes of the past we find.
Shadows linger, flickers fade,
Whispers of the dreams we made.

Pathways twist through memory's maze,
Guiding us through a hazy haze.
With each step, the echoes blend,
Tracing lines that never end.

Fragments dance upon the air,
Hints of laughter, threads of care.
In the twilight, we discern,
Lessons learned and hearts that yearn.

Journeying through the dark and light,
Finding solace in the night.
Pathways lead us to embrace,
The beauty of our inner space.

The Enigma of Clouded Visions

In the mist of dreams, we tread,
Chasing visions, softly spread.
Clouded by the night's embrace,
Seeking clarity, seeking grace.

Mysteries hide in shadows deep,
Where forgotten secrets sleep.
Through the fog, we grasp and reach,
For the truths that life may teach.

Eyes wide open, hearts aflame,
In the silence, call our name.
Unraveling what lies concealed,
With each moment, fate revealed.

Through the whispers, we perceive,
What the night is poised to weave.
Embracing all that feels unseen,
In the enigma, we glean.

Echoes of the Unseen

Whispers dance in shadowed halls,
Forgotten voices softly call.
Glimmers of light in twilight's grace,
Trace the paths we cannot face.

Haunting melodies softly play,
In the stillness of the day.
Fleeting glimpses, fading sighs,
Time dissolves as memory flies.

Beneath the surface, stories lie,
Silent truths that never die.
In the echoes, we discover,
The unseen bonds that pull us closer.

Faint reflections, dreams become,
In the heart, we find a home.
Through the night, we seek the light,
Guided by the spirits' flight.

Phantoms of the Mind

Thoughts like shadows drift and sway,
Haunted by what words can't say.
Flickering images, hard to hold,
Phantoms of tales waiting to unfold.

In the corners where fears creep,
Secrets hidden, buried deep.
Voices echo, calling me,
To face the things that never flee.

Through the labyrinth, I must roam,
Finding pieces of my home.
In the silence, clarity,
Reveals the strength inside of me.

Yet I wander, seeking light,
In the shadows of the night.
Phantoms fade as dawn draws near,
And the whispers disappear.

Daylight's Lullaby

The sun ascends with gentle rays,
Waking dreams from soft, dark haze.
Birdsong weaves a tender tune,
Bringing life to morning's bloom.

Winds embrace the trees in sway,
Nature sings the start of day.
Golden hues on petals bright,
Kissing softly, warm and light.

Every moment, pure and clear,
Whispers bring the world so near.
In the warmth, we find our peace,
Letting go, our worries cease.

Daylight's lullaby, sweet and soft,
Lifting spirits, hearts aloft.
Through the hours, let us dream,
In the glow of daylight's beam.

Dreams Wrapped in Silk

Whispers woven, delicate strands,
Capture wishes in soft hands.
Colors swirl, a gentle dance,
In the night, we find our chance.

Wrapped in silk, our dreams take flight,
Guided by the stars so bright.
Floating softly, we embrace,
Every wish, each hidden place.

Cradled by the moon's soft glow,
Timeless tales begin to flow.
Stories fragrant as the night,
In dreams, we find our true delight.

Awake, the day begins to break,
Yet in our hearts, the dreams we make.
Wrapped in silk, we hold them tight,
For in our dreams, we find the light.

Flickering Fantasies

In twilight's embrace, dreams softly rise,
Whispers of hope in the starlit skies.
Shadows entwine, in the hush of the night,
Casting our hopes in a shimmering light.

Dancing on edges of places unknown,
Flickering visions begin to be sown.
Hearts wide open, we chase the serene,
Lost in the magic of what might have been.

Every glance holds a story untold,
Moments like treasures, more precious than gold.
Through the dark veil, our spirits take flight,
Flickering dreams, guiding us through the night.

Eager for dawn, yet we linger in dreams,
Swallowed by starlight and moonlit beams.
Fantasies weave in a delicate lace,
In the quiet realm, we find our place.

The Dance of the Dusk

As daylight wanes, shadows begin to twirl,
The dance of the dusk, in a cosmic swirl.
Colors blend softly, with each fading ray,
Inviting the night to come out and play.

With whispers of breezes and secrets untold,
The stars take their positions, brave and bold.
Silhouettes sway like the leaves in the trees,
In harmony's breath, we drift with the breeze.

A symphony plays in the heart of the night,
Glow of the moon, a delicate light.
We sway in the shadows, encased in a trance,
Lost in the magic of this twilight dance.

Embraced by the dusk, we let worries go,
In the hush of the evening, we'll steal the show.
With every heartbeat, we join in the tune,
Together we dance under the blessings of moon.

Wandering Through the Ether

In the vast expanse where the whispers reside,
Ethereal paths weave, inviting the stride.
Dreamers in twilight, we float on the air,
Wandering softly, without any care.

Through realms of the mind, where visions ignite,
We traverse the unknown, guided by light.
Voices of starlight call out from afar,
Like echoes of dreams stitched into a star.

With hearts as our compass, we journey and roam,
Through nebulous waters, we've crafted our home.
Each feeling a fragment, each thought a bright spark,
Wandering aimlessly, yet never in the dark.

In this cosmic dance, where the lost find their way,
We wander through ether, by night and by day.
With every new step, more mysteries to claim,
In the tapestry woven, we find our own name.

Journeys Beyond the Gaze

Beyond the horizon, where dreams intertwine,
Journeys unfold, in a dance so divine.
With wonder as our guide, we sail through the air,
Chasing the sunset, free from despair.

Through valleys of whispers and mountains of light,
Every footstep awakens the night.
Carrying echoes of laughter and song,
In the realm of the heart, we truly belong.

The canvas of sky paints stories anew,
With colors of hope, and the promise of blue.
Our spirits unbound, we venture so far,
Journeys beyond, like a falling star.

As twilight descends, and memories fade,
We treasure the moments, the paths that we've made.
In every journey, through dusk and through dawn,
The heart finds its way, forever drawn.

Milton Keynes UK
Ingram Content Group UK Ltd.
UKHW021953151124
451186UK00007B/231